HMH SOCIAL STUDIES

HMH

AMERICAN HISTORY

RECONSTRUCTION TO THE PRESENT

Document-Based Investigation Workbook

Table of Contents

What are Document-Based Investigations (DBIs)?

A document-based investigation (DBI) requires you to use a source or a group of sources to produce a written response or some form of presentation. DBIs cannot be answered without a careful analysis of source materials. Unlike a math problem that you can work out in your head, finding the answer to a document-based investigation depends on the use of at least one outside reference.

DBIs are not as difficult as you might think. The idea is to learn to use documents as guides. Sometimes sources help you prove something you already know about a subject. At other times source materials guide you to develop a new opinion. Knowing how to examine documents is an important learning tool. Once you've mastered this skill, you will be able to draw interesting conclusions and record them in a clear and organized way.

This workbook contains 19 activities. First you will study a collection of source materials and answer short questions about each one, using the writing space provided. The documents and questions will help you develop a response to the essay or presentation topic. In the second part of the activity, you will see a prompt to which you must provide a response. You must base your response on some or all of the source materials. The prompt is called the Task and looks like this example.

> **Task**
> Explain the reasons for the rapid settlement of the West that began in the middle of the 1800s.

Further information on the Task is provided in the Historical Context. Following the Task is a set of guidelines to help you get started.

The most important things to remember about document-based investigations are:

1. to **USE THE SOURCE MATERIALS** provided. Let them guide you to an accurate and complete response.

2. to **CIRCLE, UNDERLINE, AND ANNOTATE** as you see fit. This is your workbook. Make it your own.

When you work on document-based investigations, you will analyze a variety of sources. **Primary sources** are first-hand accounts of an event, such as diaries, letters, and interviews. Primary sources also include historic documents like the Declaration of Independence and objects that have survived from the past such as coins and stamps. **Secondary sources** are accounts of past events written some time after they occurred by people who were not eyewitnesses. Your textbook or encyclopedias are examples of secondary sources.

Both types of sources can provide reliable information; both can also contain bias and inaccuracy. It is your job to judge the quality of the sources you encounter in your studies. Here are some tips.

- **Read source documents** carefully, and re-read if you don't understand the content at first. Underline words and phrases you think are important. State the main idea in your own words and write it down next to the source. When you come across difficult words or unfamiliar subjects, consult a dictionary or encyclopedia.

- **Ask questions** like "Who created the source and for what purpose?" and "How much time has passed since the source was created?" Historians use the rule of time and place to judge the reliability of source material. The closer a source and its creator were to the time and place of an event, the more reliable the source is likely to be.

- **Compare sources** with each other. Always use more than one source to confirm the accuracy of information.

- **Knowing what to expect** from a source will also help. Consider the type of document at hand. Is it a court record or a memoir, a scientific report or an ad? Did the author intend to create a private or public record? Adjust your expectations accordingly.

- **Learn to distinguish** factual information from opinions. For example, primary sources that are first-hand accounts can make a subject come alive. But they can also be one-sided because they are so personal. Look for vocabulary associated with individual points of view. Words like *personally*, *in my opinion*, or *it seemed like* can signal that the author is stating an opinion or feeling.

You actually take on the role of a historian when you work on document-based investigations. Following this step-by-step plan will help you read like a historian.

1. **Focus your reading.** In some document-based tests, students are told the subject of their essay before they begin reading the source documents. The subject may be called a task, writing prompt, or assignment. Keep this prompt in the back of your mind as you read each source.

2. **Start at the bottom!** Your smartest plan of attack is: read the source line first. Ask yourself who the author or the source of the document is. When was it written? Is it taken from a newspaper, speech, personal diary, or other source?

3. **Evaluate the writer or source.** What is the viewpoint of the author? Why is this author writing about this subject? Does the author have a goal or purpose in mind? Is the writer likely to be biased or mistaken for some reason?

4. **Identify the audience.** Who is the intended audience or user for this source? Is it the general public? If the audience is a specific group of people, who are they? What interests do they have in common?

5. **Reading a text excerpt.** If you see ellipses, or periods in a row, it means that some words or whole sentences have been taken out of an excerpt. This is usually done to shorten a document. Brackets [ ] may have been inserted. Brackets are used to show words that were not in the original document. They are used to help you better understand the information in the document.

6. **Answer the questions.** Read the short-answer questions. Expect to reread the source several times. Always use complete sentences.

7. **Refocus on the essay.** Before you move on to the next document, ask yourself: How could this information help me write the essay to come?

Prologue: American Beginnings
Document-Based Investigation

Part 1: Short Answer

In this module, you will analyze several historical documents. Carefully read or examine each document. Then answer the question that follows, citing text evidence where appropriate.

Part 2: Deliver a Presentation

Historical Context

For more than a century, people around the world have looked to the United States as a land of freedom, economic opportunity, and equality. But earning that reputation was not easy. Since colonial times, Americans have faced and overcome countless challenges in their quest to build a better society. Some of those challenges came from outside, forced upon the people by oppressive leaders or economic systems. Others, such as discrimination and social injustice, have been created by the people themselves. By overcoming these challenges, both external and internal, Americans have made their country a better place for all.

Task

Consider some of the challenges faced by the colonies and the United States in the first hundred years of its existence. Create a presentation in which you identify some of those challenges, analyze how people eventually overcame them, and explain how those efforts helped strengthen American society.

Complete the following steps as you plan and compose your presentation.

1. Review your notes and sources before you start writing.

2. Use at least *four* of the sources in Part 1, and develop the topic with relevant, well-chosen evidence from the documents.

3. Cite specific evidence from each of the sources in your response.

4. Plan your presentation so that information is delivered clearly and logically to the audience.

5. Speak clearly and with enough volume to be heard, employ relevant visuals, and use presentation technology as applicable.

6. Conclude with a summation of the main points of your presentation.

Prologue: American Beginnings

HISTORICAL SOURCE   1

Drawing of a Slave Ship

This plan and section of the British slave ship *Brookes* was published in London around 1790 by a leading British antislavery advocate named Thomas Clarkson. The image effectively conveys the degradation and inhumanity of the slave trade, which reduced human beings to the level of merchandise.

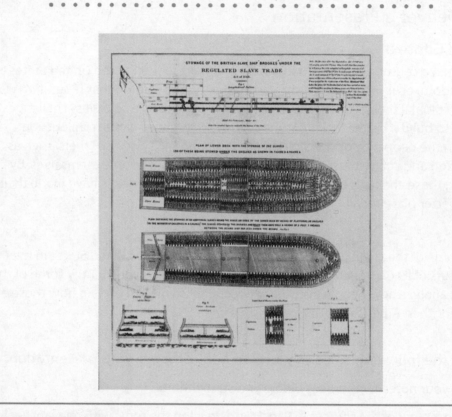

Analyze Sources

What do you think Thomas Clarkson's motive was for publishing this drawing?

Name _____ Class _____ Date _____

Mob Rule

This British cartoon portrays the events of the Boston Tea Party from the Loyalist perspective, While Patriots are dumping tea, a British tax collector, having been tarred and feathered, is having tea poured down his throat. The "Liberty Tree," where a copy of the Stamp Act has been nailed upside down, has been converted into a gallows, a device used for hanging people.

• •

Analyze Sources

What kind of comment does the cartoonist make by suspending a hangman's noose from the "Liberty Tree"? Explain.

HISTORICAL SOURCE   3

A View of the New Government

Here is John Dickinson's description of an ideal American government.

• •

"Let our government be like that of the solar system. Let the general government be like the sun and the states the planets, repelled yet attracted, and the whole moving regularly and harmoniously in their several orbits."

—John Dickinson

from *The Records of The Federal Convention of 1787*

Analyze Sources

How does Dickinson's view of the new government reflect Enlightenment ideals?

HISTORICAL SOURCE 4

Slater's Mill

This painting from around 1790 shows Samuel Slater's mill, the first cotton mill in the United States. The mill, located in Pawtucket, Rhode Island, drew its power from the Blackstone River.

• •

Analyze Sources

How does this painting illustrate the changing nature of the American economy in the 1790s?

Name _____ Class _____ Date _____

HISTORICAL SOURCE 5

Annexing Texas

Debates on the westward expansion of the United States were at the center of the 1844 presidential election. The man who would win, slaveholder James K. Polk, firmly favored annexation of Texas "at the earliest practicable period." With the annexation question settled by the time he took office in 1845, Polk again expressed his support of Texas statehood at his inauguration.

• •

"The Republic of Texas has made known her desire to come into our Union, to form a part of our Confederacy and enjoy with us the blessings of liberty secured and guaranteed by our Constitution. Texas . . . possesses an undoubted right to dispose of a part or the whole of her territory and to merge her sovereignty as a separate and independent state in ours."

—James K. Polk

from his Inaugural Address, 1845

Analyze Sources

How does Polk's statement reflect the ideas behind manifest destiny?

Document-Based Investigation Workbook

HISTORICAL SOURCE   6

The Gettysburg Address

Several months after the Battle of Gettysburg, President Lincoln spoke at a ceremony to dedicate a cemetery for those who had fallen. In a brief speech, he perfectly described the purpose of the Civil War and the ideals of American democracy.

• •

"Four score and seven years ago our fathers brought forth on this continent a new nation, conceived in Liberty, and dedicated to the proposition that all men are created equal."

Now we are engaged in a great civil war, testing whether that nation, or any nation so conceived and so dedicated, can long endure. We are met on a great battlefield of that war. We have come to dedicate a portion of that field, as a final resting place for those who here gave their lives that that nation might live. It is altogether fitting and proper that we should do this.

But, in a larger sense, we can not dedicate—we can not consecrate—we can not hallow—this ground. The brave men, living and dead, who struggled here, have consecrated it, far above our poor power to add or detract. The world will little note, nor long remember what we say here, but it can never forget what they did here. It is for us the living, rather, to be dedicated here to the unfinished work which they who fought here have thus far so nobly advanced. It is rather for us to be here dedicated to the great task remaining before us—that from these honored dead we take increased devotion to that cause for which they gave the last full measure of devotion—that we here highly resolve that these dead shall not have died in vain—that this nation, under God, shall have a new birth of freedom—and that government of the people, by the people, for the people, shall not perish from the earth."

—Abraham Lincoln

The Gettysburg Address, November 19, 1863

Analyze Sources

How does Lincoln connect the soldiers' deaths at Gettysburg to the need to continue the fight?

Name _____ Class _____ Date _____

"Unwelcome Guest"

Of all the political cartoonists of the 19th century, Thomas Nast (1840–1902) had the greatest and most long-lasting influence. This Nast cartoon from a southern Democratic newspaper depicts Carl Schurz, a liberal Republican who advocated legal equality for African Americans. Schurz is shown as a carpetbagger trudging down a dusty southern road as a crowd of people watch his arrival.

• •

THE MAN WITH THE (CARPET) BAGS.
The bag in front of him, filled with others' faults, he always sees. The one behind him, filled with his own faults, he never sees.

Analyze Sources

Is Schurz shown in a positive or negative light? How can you tell?

Westward Expansion
Document-Based Investigation

Part 1: Short Answer

In this module, you will analyze several historical documents. Carefully read or examine each document. Then answer the question that follows, citing text evidence where appropriate.

Part 2: Deliver a Presentation

Historical Context

Between 1877 and 1900, the United States went through a period of transformation. Farmers, miners, and ranchers began to settle large regions of the western United States, taking the land from Native Americans. Large businesses and new industries began to thrive and dominate the economy. Native Americans lived off of the land until they were forced to relinquish their land and culture by the incoming white Americans who wanted to farm, mine, and use the land for cattle. Settlers faced extreme hardships as they attempted to transform the land. Farmers faced further hardships as big business pushed into the West.

Task

After the end of the Civil War, groups of people began to migrate West. This migration started a ripple effect that changed the face of the frontier, slowly eroding the wilderness until the frontier disappeared entirely. Each new group moving westward struggled to impose their will on the land, fighting to be successful in using the land for their own purposes. "Success" often came at another group's expense. Prepare a presentation that explains the changes to the western frontier and the effects of those changes from the perspectives of Native Americans, ranchers, and/or farmers.

Complete the following steps as you plan and compose your presentation.

1. Review your notes and sources before you start writing.

2. Use at least *three* of the sources in Part 1, and develop the topic with relevant, well-chosen evidence from the documents.

3. Cite specific evidence from each of the sources in your response.

4. Plan your presentation so that information is delivered clearly and logically to the audience.

5. Speak clearly and with enough volume to be heard, employ relevant visuals, and use presentation technology as applicable.

6. Conclude with a summation of the main points of your presentation.

Westward Expansion

HISTORICAL SOURCE   1

Chief Satanta

Known as the Orator of the Plains, Chief Satanta represented the Kiowa people in 1867 negotiations with the U.S. government.

• •

"All the land south of the Arkansas belongs to the Kiowas and Comanches, and I don't want to give away any of it. I love the land and the buffalo and will not part with it. I want you to understand well what I say. Write it on paper. Let the Great Father [U.S. president] see it, and let me hear what he has to say. I want you to understand also, that the Kiowas and Comanches don't want to fight, and have not been fighting since we made the treaty. I hear a great deal of good talk from the gentlemen whom the Great Father sends us, but they never do what they say. I don't want any of the medicine lodges [schools and churches] within the country. I want the children raised as I was. When I make peace, it is a long and lasting one—there is no end to it. . . . A long time ago this land belonged to our fathers; but when I go up to the river I see camps of soldiers on its banks. These soldiers cut down my timber; they kill my buffalo; and when I see that, my heart feels like bursting; I feel sorry. I have spoken."

—Chief Satanta

from a speech at the Medicine Lodge Creek Council of 1867

Analyze Sources

What do Chief Satanta's words reveal about the changing frontier?

Name _____ Class _____ Date _____

HISTORICAL SOURCE   2

Changes on the Range

Teddy Abbott was born in England, but he moved to Nebraska with his family when he was ten years old. Shortly after arriving, his father bought a herd of cattle in Texas and drove the herd to Nebraska, allowing Teddy to join. Even as a young boy, he loved the life of a cowhand and continued to work as a cowboy after his father and brothers became farmers.

. . . .

"Most of southeastern Nebraska and the whole state west of Lincoln was open range when we got there in '71, but about 1876 a flock of settlers took the country, and after that there was only a few places where you could hold cattle. Father was lucky. There was a lot of rough country adjoining him that did not get settled until '79 or '80, and he run cattle until then, but afterwards he went to farming like the rest of them. That was how I come to leave home for good when I was eighteen. . . . I stayed with the cattle and went north with them. You see, environment—that's a big word for me but I got onto it—does everything for a boy. I was with cowpunchers from the time I was eleven years old. And then my father expected to make a farmer of me after that! It couldn't be done."

—Teddy Abbott

from *We Pointed Them North: Recollections of a Cowpuncher*

Analyze Sources

What does Abbott's recollection tell you about the changing frontier?

HISTORICAL SOURCE   3

Life on the Plains

Most pioneers' first homes were soddies, like the one pictured here, which were built out of bricks of sod—dense prairie grass with the roots and soil attached. This is a photograph of a pioneer   family in front of their soddy near Merna, Nebraska, in 1886.

Analyze Sources

What details in the photograph help you understand the challenges this family faced as they attempted to build a life on the plains?

HISTORICAL SOURCE   4

The Plight of the Farmers

Farmers were particularly hard hit in the decades leading to the financial panic of 1893. They regarded big business interests as insurmountable enemies who were bringing them to their knees and leaving them with debts at every turn. This cartoon is a warning of the dangers confronting not only the farmers but the entire nation.

Analyze Sources

Who does the cartoonist suggest is responsible for the farmers' plight?

Industrialization
Document-Based Investigation

Part 1: Short Answer

In this module, you will analyze several historical documents. Carefully read or examine each document. Then answer the question that follows, citing text evidence where appropriate.

Part 2: Write an Argument

Historical Context

In the late 1800s, few laws applied to big businesses, including the railroads. As a result, powerful businesses and business owners were able to use unfair practices to dominate American industry. This domination was not only bad for consumers, but also for workers. Consumers pushed for more government regulation, and workers formed labor unions to fight for improved working conditions and pay. However, the wealth and influence of big business made for a difficult opponent to defeat.

Task

Industrialization raised living standards and made many business owners wealthy. However, many Americans were still desperately poor. In 1899, women earned an average of $267 a year, nearly half of men's average pay of $498. In contrast, Andrew Carnegie made $23 million, with no income tax, in 1900. Write an argument against the growing wealth and influence of big business. Focus on unfair business practices, exploitative practices towards workers, government corruption, and loose laws and regulations.

Complete the following steps as you plan and compose your argument.

1. Review your notes and sources before you start writing.

2. Use at least *three* of the sources in Part 1, and develop the topic with relevant, well-chosen evidence from the documents.

3. Cite specific evidence from each of the sources in your response.

4. Plan your argument so that it includes an introduction, body paragraphs with supporting details, and a concluding paragraph.

5. Organize your argument in a clear and logical way that expresses your point of view to the reader.

6. Write a conclusion that sums up your ideas and supports the information you present.

Industrialization

The Brooklyn Bridge

It took 600 workers 14 years to complete the Brooklyn Bridge at a cost of about $320 million in today's dollars. The opening ceremony took place on May 24, 1883. That first day, about 250,000 pedestrians crossed the bridge.

· ·

In 1883, upon its completion, the Brooklyn Bridge was the longest suspension bridge in the world.

Today, thousands of commuters use the bridge every day, including more than 100,000 cars, 4,000 pedestrians, and 3,000 bicyclists.

Analyze Sources

Compare the photographs. How is the Brooklyn Bridge of 1894 similar to the Brooklyn Bridge of 1980?

HISTORICAL SOURCE   2

"The Modern Colossus of (Rail) Roads"

Joseph Keppler drew this cartoon in 1879. The title is a pun on the *Colossus of Rhodes*, a statue erected in 282 BCE on an island near Greece. According to legend, the 100-foot-tall statue straddled Rhodes's harbor entrance.

• •

The central figure is railroad "giant" William Vanderbilt, who is using strings like a puppetmaster to control the movements of the railroad networks.

The figure attached to Vanderbilt's right leg is Cyrus W. Fields. After Fields's company successfully laid a transatlantic telegraph cable in 1866, he turned his attention and wealth elsewhere, working with Jay Gould to develop railroad networks.

THE MODERN COLOSSUS OF (RAIL) ROADS.

The figure attached to Vanderbilt's left leg is railroad magnate Jay Gould. By 1881 Gould controlled more than 15,000 miles of track, which was about 15 percent of the railroad network in the United States.

Analyze Sources

The reins held by the railroad magnates attach not only to the trains but also to the tracks and the railroad station. What does this convey about the magnates' control of the railroads?

Document-Based Investigation Workbook

HISTORICAL SOURCE   3

"What a Funny Little Government!"

This 1900 cartoon—captioned "What a funny little government!"—is a commentary on the power of American industrialists.

The large figure in the foreground is John D. Rockefeller.

Factory smokestacks lie behind the U.S. Capitol, pumping black smoke into the air.

Rockefeller holds the White House in the palm of his hand.

Analyze Sources

What is the cartoonist suggesting by showing the White House in the hands of a tycoon like Rockefeller?

HISTORICAL SOURCE 4

Sweatshops

In sweatshops, or workshops in tenements rather than in factories, workers had little choice but to put up with the conditions. Sweatshop employment, which was tedious and required few skills, was often the only avenue open to women and children. Jacob Riis described the conditions faced by "sweaters."

• •

"The bulk of the sweater's work is done in the tenements, which the law that regulates factory labor does not reach. . . . In [them] the child works unchallenged from the day he is old enough to pull a thread. There is no such thing as a dinner hour; men and women eat while they work, and the 'day' is lengthened at both ends far into the night."

—Jacob Riis

from *How the Other Half Lives*

Analyze Sources

According to Jacob Riis, how were working conditions for children in sweatshops?

Immigration and Urbanization
Document-Based Investigation

Part 1: Short Answer

In this module, you will analyze several historical documents. Carefully read or examine each document. Then answer the question that follows, citing text evidence where appropriate.

Part 2: Deliver a Presentation

Historical Context

The later half of the 19th century saw a wave of immigration to the United States from Europe and Asia. Many of these immigrants settled in cities on the East and West coasts, contributing to rapid urbanization. With rapid urbanization came problems, such as overcrowding. Advances in science, technology, and urban planning help solve some urban problems. Other problems, such as political corruption, were harder to solve.

Task

The turn of the century was a dynamic period in the history of the United States. It saw a massive influx of immigrants and the growth of modern cities. It was also a time of rapid advances in technology and of rampant political corruption. Plan and deliver a presentation in which you discuss the major themes of the time period, highlighting key people, ideas, innovations, and events. Focus on the themes of immigration, urbanization, innovation, and political corruption.

Complete the following steps as you plan and prepare your presentation.

1. Review your notes and sources before you start writing.

2. Use at least *four* of the sources in Part 1, and develop the topic with relevant, well-chosen evidence from the documents.

3. Cite specific evidence from each of the sources in your response.

4. Plan your presentation so that information is delivered clearly and logically to the audience.

5. Speak clearly and with enough volume to be heard, employ relevant visuals, and use presentation technology as applicable.

6. Conclude with a summation of the main points of your presentation.

Immigration and Urbanization

HISTORICAL SOURCE 1

Immigration

Immigrants faced difficult and sometimes dangerous conditions just to make it to Ellis Island or Angel Island. However, there still was no guarantee that they would be admitted into the United States.

• •

★

"*America!* . . . We were so near it seemed too much to believe. Everyone stood silent—like in prayer. . . . Then we were entering the harbor. The land came so near we could almost reach out and touch it. . . . Everyone was holding their breath. Me too. . . . Some boats had bands playing on their decks and all of them were tooting their horns to us and leaving white trails in the water behind them."

—Rosa Cavalleri

quoted in *Rosa: The Life of an Italian Immigrant*

"When I saw Ellis Island, it's a great big place, . . . We all had to gather your bags, and the place was crowded with people and talking, and crying, . . . And we passed through some of the halls there, big open spaces there, and there was bars, and there was people behind these bars, and they were talking different languages, and I was scared to death. I thought I was in jail."

—Mary Mullins Gordon

quoted in *Ellis Island Oral History Project*

Analyze Sources

How was the experience of arriving in the United States different for Rosa Cavalleri and Mary Mullins Gordon?

Document-Based Investigation Workbook

HISTORICAL SOURCE   2

The San Francisco Earthquake of 1906

At 5:12 on the morning of April 18, 1906, while many in the city slept, a massive earthquake struck San Francisco, California. The force of the earthquake and the fires that followed destroyed much of the city. Jack London described the fires that raged after the earthquake.

• •

"On Wednesday morning at a quarter past five came the earthquake. A minute later the flames were leaping upward. In a dozen different quarters south of Market Street, in the working-class ghetto, and in the factories, fires started. There was no opposing the flames. . . . And the great water-mains had burst. All the shrewd contrivances and safeguards of man had been thrown out of gear by thirty seconds' twitching of the earth-crust."

—Jack London

from "The Story of an Eye-witness"

Analyze Sources

According to Jack London, how did the earthquake undo the safeguards the city had put into place to fight fires?

HISTORICAL SOURCE   3

"The Tammany Tiger Loose"

Political cartoonist Thomas Nast ridiculed Boss Tweed and his machine in the pages of *Harper's Weekly*. Nast's work threatened Tweed, who reportedly said, "I don't care so much what the papers write about me—my constituents can't read; but . . . they can see pictures!"

• •

Boss Tweed and his cronies are portrayed as noblemen, watching from the stands.

The tiger represents the Tammany Hall political machine. Thomas Nast seems to be suggesting that Tammany, like a tiger, is a fierce, unstoppable beast.

Under the Tammany tiger's victim is a torn paper that reads "LAW." The cartoon's caption reads: "What are you going to do about it?"

Analyze Sources

What effect do you think Nast wanted this political cartoon to have on his audience?

HISTORICAL SOURCE   4

The Wright Flyer

The Wright Flyer had a wooden frame covered in canvas. It measured 9 feet 4 inches high and just over 21 feet long, with a wingspan of 40 feet 4 inches. Powered by a 4-cylinder 12-horsepower piston engine, the total weight of the airplane was 605 pounds. The engine, at 180 pounds, was the heaviest component in the airplane. The design of lighter, more powerful engines was the most important development in early aviation history.

• •

Analyze Sources

Examine the photos of the Wright Flyer and its engine. Why do you think the Wright brothers did not paint their airplane?

HISTORICAL SOURCE 5

Realism

This 1871 painting, *The Champion Single Sculls (Max Schmitt In A Single Scull)*, by Thomas Eakins is an example of the realist movement. This artistic school focused on representing people and environments as they really are.

Analyze Sources

What realistic details do you see portrayed in this painting?

Progressivism
Document-Based Investigation

Part 1: Short Answer

In this module, you will analyze several historical documents. Carefully read or examine each document. Then answer the question that follows, citing text evidence where appropriate.

Part 2: Write a Compare-and-Contrast Essay

Historical Context

The progressive movement responded to a growing public demand for government to become involved in social, political, and economic reform. Although progressivism was not a single movement, the aim of progressive reformers was to restore economic opportunities and correct injustices in American life. It was an effort to redress imbalances, or curb excesses, that had arisen in the period of rapid industrial growth and national expansion following the Civil War.

Task

Progressive reformers tried to address and solve a number of problems—economic, political, and social. Often, reformers never completely agreed on the problems, let alone the solutions. However, they were still able to enact a number of successful and needed reforms. In which arena—social, political, or economic—do you think progressive reforms were the most successful? Write an essay to compare and contrast the successes of reforms in different progressive arenas. Conclude your essay by stating in which arena you feel progressives were the most successful.

Complete the following steps as you plan and compose your compare-and-contrast essay.

1. Review your notes and sources before you start writing.

2. Use at least *four* of the sources in Part 1, and develop the topic with relevant, well-chosen evidence from the documents.

3. Cite specific evidence from each of the sources in your response.

4. Plan your compare-and-contrast essay so that it includes an introduction, several body paragraphs, and a concluding paragraph.

5. Organize your essay in a clear and logical way that highlights the similarities and differences among sources.

6. Write a conclusion that sums up your ideas and supports the information you present.

Progressivism

HISTORICAL SOURCE   1

Lewis Hine

In 1908 Lewis Hine quit his teaching job to document child labor practices. He believed in the power of photography to move people to action. His compelling images of exploitation—such as these spindle boys and girls who were forced to climb atop moving machinery to replace parts—helped to convince the public of the need for child labor regulations.

Hine devised a host of clever tactics to gain access to his subjects. He learned shop managers' schedules and arrived during their lunch breaks. While talking casually with the children, he secretly scribbled notes on paper hidden in his pocket.

• •

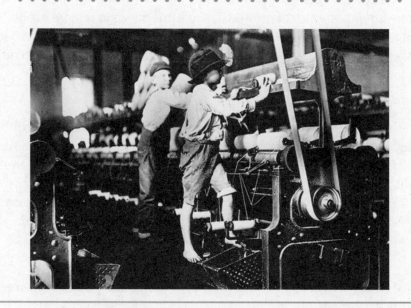

Analyze Sources

What elements of this photograph do you find most striking?

HISTORICAL SOURCE 2

Early Immigrant Education

By 1895 most states passed laws requiring children under age 14 to attend school. One 13-year-old boy explained to a Chicago school inspector why he hid in a warehouse basement instead of going to school.

• •

"They hits ye if yer don't learn, and they hits ye if ye whisper, and they hits ye if ye have string in yer pocket, and they hits ye if yer seat squeaks, and they hits ye if ye don't stan' up in time, and they hits ye if yer late, and they hits ye if ye ferget the page."

—anonymous schoolboy

quoted in *The One Best System*

Analyze Sources

What reason does the Chicago schoolboy give for not wanting to attend school?

HISTORICAL SOURCE   3

The Atlanta Compromise

On September 18, 1895, Booker T. Washington was invited to deliver a speech to the Cotton States and International Exposition in Atlanta. In the speech, he outlined his ideas about racial inequality and the shared responsibilities of African Americans and whites in improving society both socially and economically.

• •

"To those of the white race . . . I would repeat what I say to my own race. . . . Cast down your bucket among these people who have, without strikes and labour wars, tilled your fields, cleared your forests, built your railroads and cities, and brought forth treasures from the bowels of the earth. . . . In all things that are purely social we can be as separate as the fingers, yet one as the hand in all things essential to mutual progress."

—Booker T. Washington

from a speech to the Cotton States and International Exposition

Analyze Sources

How do Washington's words represent a compromise?

HISTORICAL SOURCE 4

Educational Opportunities

Although women were still expected to fulfill traditional domestic roles, women's colleges sought to grant women an excellent education. In her will, Smith College's founder, Sophia Smith, made her goals clear.

• •

"[It is my desire] to furnish for my own sex means and facilities for education equal to those which are afforded now in our College to young men. . . . It is not my design to render my sex any the less feminine, but to develop as fully as may be the powers of womanhood & furnish women with means of usefulness, happiness, & honor now withheld from them."

—Sophia Smith

quoted in *Alma Mater*

Analyze Sources

What do you think Sophia Smith hoped women would be able to accomplish through higher education?

HISTORICAL SOURCE 5

"The Lion-Tamer"

As part of his Square Deal, President Roosevelt aggressively used the Sherman Antitrust Act of 1890 to attack big businesses engaging in unfair practices. His victory over the Northern Securities Company earned him a reputation as a hard-hitting trustbuster committed to protecting the public interest.

• •

The lions are entering the arena from a door labeled "Wall Street."

Teddy Roosevelt stands fearlessly amongst the lions, taming them with a whip.

The wild lions symbolize powerful businesses and trusts in 1904.

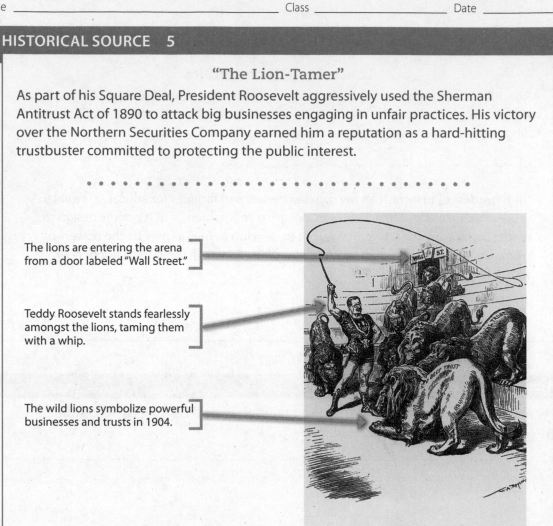

Analyze Sources

What do you think is the cartoonist's opinion of Roosevelt? Cite details from the cartoon that support your interpretation.

HISTORICAL SOURCE 6

"Such a Sad Case!"

Progressives in the Republican Party were angered by Taft's support of the Payne-Aldrich Tariff. Many felt that it not only hurt American consumers, but also weakened American industry.

• •

Toys representing political parties are on the tray of the walker. The Republican elephant is broken.

American industry is represented by a toddler, unable to walk without support.

American industry is also fed by a bottle of "Payne Aldrich Baby Food."

SUCH A SAD CASE!
His Delusion Is That He Cannot Walk Alone.

Analyze Sources

What is the cartoonist suggesting about the effects of the Payne-Aldrich Tariff on American industry?

HISTORICAL SOURCE   7

Suffrage Prisoners

Some suffragists favored stronger forms of protest, which sometimes landed them in jail. This young woman is protesting the rough treatment received by these suffragists at the hands of the police and other government officials.

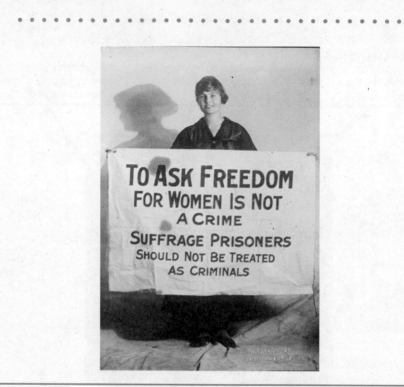

Analyze Sources

What does the young woman's sign suggest about the treatment of those fighting for woman suffrage?

Document-Based Investigation Workbook

U.S. Imperialism
Document-Based Investigation

Part 1: Short Answer

In this module, you will analyze several historical documents. Carefully read or examine each document. Then answer the question that follows, citing text evidence where appropriate.

Part 2: Write an Explanatory Essay

Historical Context

The late 1800s are often referred to as the "Age of Imperialism." The United States joined other nations in pursuit of power and influence around the world. U.S. imperialist desires were influence by a number of cultural, economic, and political factors. Advances in technology also helped to fuel U.S. imperialism. Mechanization of farming and manufacturing increased the production of goods, prompting the need to find overseas markets.

Task

Many Americans were in favor of U.S. imperialism and the growing influence of the United States around the world. Other Americans, however, took a more cautious approach toward the growing involvement of the United States in world affairs. Write an explanatory essay to summarize the positions of interventionists and non-interventionists with respect to U.S. imperialism and foreign policy.

Complete the following steps as you plan and compose your explanatory essay.

1. Review your notes and sources before you start writing.

2. Use at least *three* of the sources in Part 1, and develop the topic with relevant, well-chosen evidence from the documents.

3. Cite specific evidence from each of the sources in your response.

4. Plan your explanatory essay so that it includes an introduction, several body paragraphs, and a concluding paragraph.

5. Organize your essay in a clear and logical way that provides a detailed explanation of the topic.

6. Write a conclusion that sums up your ideas and supports the information you present.

U.S. Imperialism

HISTORICAL SOURCE   1

Buying and Selling Alaska

While leaders in the United States government debated whether to buy Alaska, Russian officials were having a similar debate about the sale of their colony.

• •

"In view of the straitened circumstances of State finances . . . I think we would do well to take advantage of the excess of money . . . in the Treasury of the United States of America and to sell our North American colonies. . . . we must not deceive ourselves and must forsee that the United States, . . . desiring to dominate undividedly the whole of North America, will take the . . . colonies from us and we shall not be able to regain them. . . . At the same time these colonies bring us very small profit and their loss to us would not be greatly felt. . . . These considerations I beg Your Excellency to report to His Majesty the Emperor."

—Grand Duke Konstantin

from a letter to Prince A. M. Gorchakov, March 22, 1857

Analyze Sources

What reservations does Grand Duke Konstantin have about the United States' interest in Alaska?

HISTORICAL SOURCE 2

Interventionists vs. Noninterventionists

The issue of whether to annex the Philippines was part of a larger debate about U.S. imperialism. The novelist and anti-imperialist Mark Twain questioned the motives for U.S. intervention around the world in a satirical piece written in 1901. At a meeting of the Republican Party, Indiana senator Albert Beveridge made a case in favor of global intervention

★

Mark Twain

"Shall we go on conferring our Civilization upon the peoples that sit in darkness, or shall we give those poor things a rest? . . . Extending the Blessings of Civilization to our Brother who Sits in Darkness has been a good trade and has paid well, on the whole; and there is money in it yet . . . but not enough, in my judgment, to make any considerable risk advisable."

—Mark Twain

quoted in *To the Person Sitting in Darkness*

Albert Beveridge

"The Opposition tells us that we ought not to govern a people without their consent. . . . Would not the people of the Philippines prefer the just, humane, civilizing government of this Republic to the savage, bloody rule of pillage and extortion from which we have rescued them? Do not the blazing fires of joy and the ringing bells of gladness in Porto Rico prove the welcome of our flag? . . . do we owe no duty to the world? . . . Shall we abandon them, with Germany, England, Japan, hungering for them?"

—Albert Beveridge

from the March of the Flag speech, September 16, 1898

Analyze Sources

What reasons does Beveridge give for a foreign policy of intervention? Why do you think Twain opposes intervention?

HISTORICAL SOURCE   3

U.S. Intervention

Throughout the early 1900s, the United States intervened in the affairs of its Latin American neighbors several times. Not surprisingly, few Latin Americans welcomed United States intervention. As the cartoon shows, the United States had a different point of view.

The imperialist's bill of fare, or menu, shows different countries and territories on offer to Uncle Sam.

President William McKinley is the waiter taking Uncle Sam's order.

Uncle Sam is seated at a dining table in a restaurant.

WELL, I HARDLY KNOW WHICH TO TAKE FIRST!

Analyze Sources

What seems to be Uncle Sam's attitude toward the offerings on the menu?

HISTORICAL SOURCE 4

"The World's Constable"

This cartoon, drawn by Louis Dalrymple in 1905, shows Teddy Roosevelt implementing his new world diplomacy. The cartoon implies that Roosevelt has the right to execute police power to keep the countries of Europe out of the affairs of Latin American countries.

• •

Roosevelt is carrying a club marked "the new diplomacy." The Roosevelt Corollary warned that the United States would "exercise international police powers" in Latin America, if necessary.

Teddy Roosevelt is shown as a constable, or police officer, indicating his willingness to aid the rest of the world. The paper in his belt reads, "Tell your troubles to the policeman."

Roosevelt has a paper labeled "arbitration" tucked under one arm. As president, he helped arbitrate peace in such international conflicts as a war between Russia and Japan. Representatives of both countries appear on the right side of the cartoon.

Figures representing Latin America and the Philippines, who borrowed from European banks, appeal to the figure of Roosevelt for assistance.

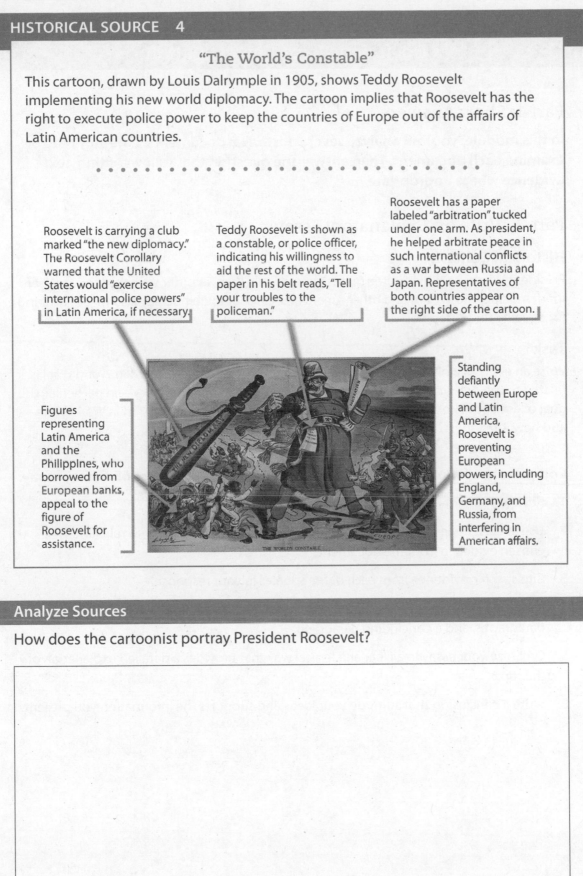

THE WORLD'S CONSTABLE

Standing defiantly between Europe and Latin America, Roosevelt is preventing European powers, including England, Germany, and Russia, from interfering in American affairs.

Analyze Sources

How does the cartoonist portray President Roosevelt?

World War I
Document-Based Investigation

Part 1: Short Answer

In this module, you will analyze several historical documents. Carefully read or examine each document. Then answer the question that follows, citing text evidence where appropriate.

Part 2: Write an Explanatory Essay

Historical Context

President Wilson said the United States joined World War I in order to make the word "safe for democracy." To Wilson and other Americans, extending democracy also meant aspiring for equality for all people.

Task

Write an essay in which you explain how the United States' involvement in World War I is related to the American mission of protecting the virtues of democracy—in particular, the goal of equality. Explain how the United States succeeded in this mission in World War I and how it fell short.

Complete the following steps as you plan and compose your explanatory essay.

1. Review your notes and sources before you start writing.

2. Use at least *three* of the sources in Part 1, and develop the topic with relevant, well-chosen evidence from the documents.

3. Cite specific evidence from each of the sources in your response.

4. Plan your explanatory essay so that it includes an introduction, several body paragraphs, and a concluding paragraph.

5. Organize your essay in a clear and logical way that provides a detailed explanation of the topic.

6. Write a conclusion that sums up your ideas and supports the information you present.

World War I

HISTORICAL SOURCE   1

"Peace Without Victory"

After the 1916 election, President Wilson tried to mediate between the warring alliances in Europe. The attempt failed. In a later speech, the president asked the Allied and Central powers to accept a "peace without victory," in which neither side would impose harsh terms on the other.

· ·

"The treaties and agreements which bring [the war] to an end must embody terms which will create a peace that is worth guaranteeing and preserving, a peace that will win the approval of mankind, not merely a peace that will serve the several interests and immediate aims of the nations engaged. . . . it must be a peace without victory . . . Victory would mean peace forced upon the loser, a victor's terms imposed upon the vanquished. It would be accepted in humiliation, under duress, at an intolerable sacrifice, and would leave a sting, a resentment, a bitter memory upon which terms of peace would rest, not permanently, but only as upon quicksand. Only a peace between equals can last."

—President Woodrow Wilson

from an address to the Senate, January 22, 1917

Analyze Sources

How does this speech reflect Wilson's ideas about equality in a postwar world?

HISTORICAL SOURCE   2

Uncle Sam the Recruiter

Before motion pictures and television were commonplace, the poster was an important visual medium. Easily produced and displayed, posters captured the immediate attention of the public.

In an effort to increase military recruitment, the U.S. government hired artists to create posters to appeal to a sense of patriotism in young men. James Montgomery Flagg's portrayal of a stern Uncle Sam became the most famous recruiting poster in American history.

· ·

Analyze Sources

How effective do you think the poster was in convincing men to fight for the Allied cause?

HISTORICAL SOURCE 3

African American Support of the War

W.E.B. Du Bois believed that African American support for the war would strengthen calls for racial justice. Du Bois explained his position.

• •

"That which the German power represents today spells death to the aspirations of Negroes and all darker races for equality, freedom and democracy. . . . Let us, while this war lasts, forget our special grievances and close our ranks shoulder to shoulder with our own white fellow citizens and the allied nations that are fighting for democracy."

—W.E.B. Du Bois

from "Close Ranks"

Analyze Sources

How does Du Bois try to convince African Americans to support the war effort?

HISTORICAL SOURCE 4

The Fourteen Points

In addition to outlining specific proposals for peace, the Fourteen Points marked a new philosophy—that the foreign policy of a democratic nation should be based on a sense of morality, not just national interests.

• •

"We entered this war because violations of right had occurred which touched us to the quick and made the life of our own people impossible unless they were corrected and the world secured once for all against their recurrence. What we demand in this war, therefore, is nothing peculiar to ourselves. It is that the world be made fit and safe to live in; and particularly that it be made safe for every peace-loving nation which, like our own, wishes to live its own life, determine its own institutions, be assured of justice and fair dealing by the other peoples of the world as against force and selfish aggression."

—Woodrow Wilson

from the "Fourteen Points"

Analyze Sources

How do Wilson's ideas for foreign policy in the Fourteen Points reflect the same democratic ideas expressed in the nation's founding documents?

The Roaring Twenties
Document-Based Investigation

Part 1: Short Answer

In this module, you will analyze several historical documents. Carefully read or examine each document. Then answer the question that follows, citing text evidence where appropriate.

Part 2: Write an Analytical Essay

Historical Context

The shock of World War I left many Americans exhausted and anxious for the return of good times. And return they did, as business boomed and people found new ways to have fun. But a grim side to American society also thrived.

Task

During the Roaring Twenties the United States was caught up in a frenzy of both fun and conflict. Write an essay in which you analyze why a historian might describe the era as a marble temple built on sand. Think about what the marble temple and the sand might represent and about how these aspects of 1920s American society might influence future events.

Complete the following steps as you plan and compose your analytical essay.

1. Review your notes and sources before you start writing.

2. Use at least *four* of the sources in Part 1, and develop the topic with relevant, well-chosen evidence from the documents.

3. Cite specific evidence from each of the sources in your response.

4. Plan your analytical essay so that it includes an introduction, body paragraphs with supporting details, and a concluding paragraph.

5. Organize your essay in a clear and logical way that presents a detailed analysis of the topic.

6. Write a conclusion that sums up your ideas and supports the information you present.

The Roaring Twenties

HISTORICAL SOURCE   1

Coolidge and Big Business

This cartoon depicts Calvin Coolidge playing a saxophone labeled "Praise" while a woman representing "Big Business" dances and sings "Yes, Sir, He's My Baby."

• •

Analyze Sources

What do you think the cartoonist suggests about Coolidge's relationship with big business?

Document-Based Investigation Workbook

HISTORICAL SOURCE 2

Palmer and the Red Scare

As fear of Communists spread, Palmer expressed the panic that many Americans felt.

• •

"The blaze of revolution was sweeping over every American institution of law and order . . . eating its way into the homes of the American workman, its sharp tongues of revolutionary heat . . . licking the altars of the churches, leaping into the belfry of the school bell, crawling into the sacred corners of American homes, . . . burning up the foundations of society."

—A. Mitchell Palmer

from "The Case Against the Reds"

Analyze Sources

What are some words and phrases that Palmer used to stir up emotions? Why do you think Palmer didn't provide any evidence of his claims?

HISTORICAL SOURCE 3

Al Capone in Chicago

By age 26, Al Capone headed a criminal empire in Chicago, which he controlled through the use of bribes and violence. He bootlegged whiskey from Canada, operated illegal breweries in Chicago, and ran a network of 10,000 speakeasies. In 1940 writer Herbert Asbury recalled the Capone era in Chicago.

• •

"The famous seven-ton armored car, with the pudgy gangster lolling on silken cushions in its darkened recesses, a big cigar in his fat face, and a $50,000 diamond ring blazing from his left hand, was one of the sights of the city; the average tourist felt that his trip to Chicago was a failure unless it included a view of Capone out for a spin. The mere whisper: 'Here comes Al,' was sufficient to stop traffic and to set thousands of curious citizens craning their necks along the curbing."

—Herbert Asbury

from *Gem of the Prairie*

Analyze Sources

How does Capone's reputation reflect attitudes about Prohibition?

HISTORICAL SOURCE 4

Working-Class Women in the 1920s

Helen Wright, who worked for the Women's Bureau in Chicago, recorded the struggle of an Irish mother of two.

• •

"She worked in one of the meat-packing companies, pasting labels from 7 a.m. to 3:30 p.m. She had entered the eldest child at school but sent her to the nursery for lunch and after school. The youngest was in the nursery all day. She kept her house 'immaculately clean and in perfect order,' but to do so worked until eleven o'clock every night in the week and on Saturday night she worked until five o'clock in the morning. She described her schedule as follows: on Tuesday, Wednesday, Thursday, and Friday she cleaned one room each night; Saturday afternoon she finished the cleaning and put the house in order; Saturday night she washed; Sunday she baked; Monday night she ironed."

—Helen Wright

quoted in *Wage–Earning Women*

Analyze Sources

How does the woman described in this account reflect the contradicting expectations women experienced during the 1920s?

HISTORICAL SOURCE 5

A Businessman Changes His Suit

One of the defining novels of the 1920s, Sinclair Lewis's *Babbitt* is a blistering satire of American culture. Set in a fictional Midwestern city named Zenith, the novel pokes fun at the empty shallowness of the booster clubs and lodges where deals were made and social status was measured.

• •

"A sensational event was changing from the brown suit to the gray the contents of his pockets. He was earnest about these objects. They were of eternal importance, like baseball or the Republican Party. They included a fountain pen and a silver pencil . . . which belonged in the righthand upper vest pocket. Without them he would have felt naked. On his watch-chain were a gold penknife, silver cigar-cutter, seven keys . . . and incidentally a good watch. . . . Last, he stuck in his lapel the Boosters' Club button. With the conciseness of great art the button displayed two words: 'Boosters—Pep!'"

—Sinclair Lewis

from *Babbitt*

Analyze Sources

For what was Sinclair Lewis ridiculing Americans?

HISTORICAL SOURCE   6

Marcus Garvey on the Rights of African Americans

The UNIA claimed four million members, although that figure has been disputed. What is certain, though, is that Garvey's message appealed both to many African Americans and to numerous black people around the world.

• •

"In view of the fact that the black man of Africa has contributed as much to the world as the white man of Europe, and the brown man and yellow man of Asia, we of the Universal Negro Improvement Association demand that the white, yellow, and brown races give to the black man his place in the civilization of the world. We ask for nothing more than the rights of 400 million Negroes."

—Marcus Garvey

from a speech at Liberty Hall, New York City, 1922

Analyze Sources

How do you think reactions to Garvey's speech might have varied among the audience members?

Name _____ Class _____ Date _____

The Great Depression
Document-Based Investigation

Part 1: Short Answer

In this module, you will analyze several historical documents. Carefully read or examine each document. Then answer the question that follows, citing text evidence where appropriate.

Part 2: Write an Explanatory Essay

Historical Context

The Great Depression was an economic disaster that struck countries around the world. In the United States it affected many aspects of Americans' lives. It also shook Americans' confidence in the future.

Task

Although the Great Depression was basically an economic disaster, it was much more than that. Write an explanatory essay in which you explain what made the Great Depression more than an economic problem. Think about the cascading effects of the economic issues on people's lives and how they responded.

Complete the following steps as you plan and compose your explanatory essay.

1. Review your notes and sources before you start writing.

2. Use *three* of the sources in Part 1, and develop the topic with relevant, well-chosen evidence from the documents.

3. Cite specific evidence from each of the sources in your response.

4. Plan your explanatory essay so that it includes an introduction, body paragraphs with supporting details, and a concluding paragraph.

5. Organize your essay in a clear and logical way that presents a detailed explanation of the topic.

6. Write a conclusion that sums up your ideas and supports the information you present.

The Great Depression

HISTORICAL SOURCE 1

Day of Wrath

After the apparent prosperity of the 1920s, few Americans were prepared for the devastating effects of the stock market crash. This cartoon by James N. Rosenberg, which shows Wall Street crumbling on October 29, 1929, is titled *Dies Irae,* Latin for "day of wrath." "Dies Irae" is also the title of a sequence in the Roman Catholic *Mass For The Dead* that describes the final judgment at the end of the world.

· ·

Analyze Sources

Why do you think the cartoonist used the title *Dies Irae?*

HISTORICAL SOURCE   2

The Hoboes

Novelist Thomas Wolfe described a group of hoboes in New York City.

• •

"These were the wanderers from town to town, the riders of freight trains, the thumbers of rides on highways, the uprooted, unwanted male population of America. They . . . gathered in the big cities when winter came, hungry, defeated, empty, hopeless, restless . . . always on the move, looking everywhere for work, for the bare crumbs to support their miserable lives, and finding neither work nor crumbs."

—Thomas Wolfe

from *You Can't Go Home Again*

Analyze Sources

Why do you think the men that Wolfe described were so stunned by their poverty? How might the despair of these men have affected those who witnessed their misery?

HISTORICAL SOURCE   3

Carrying the Weight of the Depression

In this cartoon, both farmers and President Hoover are carrying heavy loads. The caption plays on the two different meanings of the word *credit*.

Analyze Sources

What does the cartoonist suggest that the farmers and Hoover should do?

The New Deal
Document-Based Investigation

Part 1: Short Answer

In this module, you will analyze several historical documents. Carefully read or examine each document. Then answer the question that follows, citing text evidence where appropriate.

Part 2: Write an Analytical Essay

Historical Context

President Roosevelt's plan for economic recovery involved a combination of financial reforms, work programs, and social welfare programs.

Task

Write an essay in which you analyze why a combination of different forms of relief and reform would be more effective for economic recovery than just one type of solution. Consider why Roosevelt may have preferred work programs to welfare.

Complete the following steps as you plan and compose your analytical essay.

1. Review your notes and sources before you start writing.

2. Use at least *four* of the sources in Part 1, and develop the topic with relevant, well-chosen evidence from the documents.

3. Cite specific evidence from each of the sources in your response.

4. Plan your analytical essay so that it includes an introduction, body paragraphs with supporting details, and a concluding paragraph.

5. Organize your essay in a clear and logical way that presents a detailed analysis of the topic.

6. Write a conclusion that sums up your ideas and supports the information you present.

The New Deal

HISTORICAL SOURCE   1

First Fireside Chat

In this first fireside chat, President Roosevelt encouraged Americans not to lose faith in the banking system and stressed the vital role of banks in maintaining the American way of life. His address had a tremendous impact on national morale. When the banks reopened, the expected panic did not materialize.

"When you deposit money in a bank the bank does not put the money into a safe deposit vault. It invests your money . . . to keep the wheels of industry and agriculture turning around. A comparatively small part of the money that you put into the bank is kept in currency—an amount which in normal times is wholly sufficient to cover the cash needs of the average citizen. . . . Some of our bankers had shown themselves either incompetent or dishonest in the handling of the people's funds. . . . And so it became the Government's job to straighten out this situation and do it as quickly as possible."

—Franklin D. Roosevelt

from a Fireside Chat, March 12, 1933

Analyze Sources

According to Roosevelt, why is the money invested in banks important to the U.S. economy?

HISTORICAL SOURCE   2

"Migrant Mother" (1936), Dorothea Lange

In February 1936 Resettlement Administration photographer Dorothea Lange visited a camp of destitute pea pickers in Nipomo, California. One of Lange's photographs documenting the harsh living conditions, "Migrant Mother," was published in the *San Francisco News* on March 10, 1936. The photograph became one of the most recognizable symbols of the Depression and perhaps the strongest argument in support of New Deal relief programs.

• •

"I saw and approached the hungry and desperate mother, as if drawn by a magnet. . . . She said that they had been living on frozen vegetables from the surrounding fields, and birds that the children killed. She had just sold the tires from her car to buy food."

—Dorothea Lange

Analyze Sources

Why do you think "Migrant Mother" was effective in persuading people to support FDR's relief programs?

Name _____ Class _____ Date _____

HISTORICAL SOURCE   3

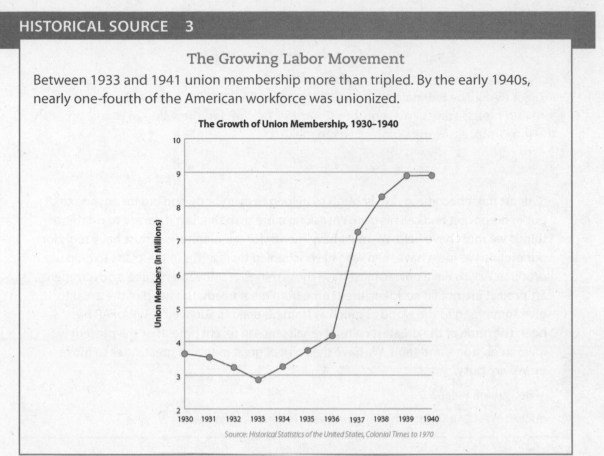

The Growing Labor Movement

Between 1933 and 1941 union membership more than tripled. By the early 1940s, nearly one-fourth of the American workforce was unionized.

The Growth of Union Membership, 1930–1940

Source: *Historical Statistics of the United States, Colonial Times to 1970*

Analyze Sources

What years on the graph show the sharpest increase in union membership?

HISTORICAL SOURCE 4

"For the Present We Are Busy"

Sculptor Beniamino Benvenuto Bufano received assistance through the Federal Art Project (FAP). The FAP paid for his studio space in San Francisco, as well as a salary for him and his assistants. In a report to Congress, he stressed the value of public art and the importance of supporting artists to make it.

• •

"Our art must become . . . big enough to belong to everybody, too big for anyone to put in his pocket and call his own. We ask no more than this, but if we are to do these things we must have help. We must have money for our granite, we must have tools for our metals. We must have men who have schooled themselves in the crafts to help us produce. Art, to have power, must have these things. . . . Movements like a government art project are not an accident; they come from great needs, the need of the artist to give something to the world as much as from his need to survive. . . . WPA/FAP has been the hope of the greatest cultural renaissance in recent times. For the present we have steel, stone, and tools. We have the spirit of great men and great cities to move us. We are busy."

—Beniamino Bufano

quoted in *Federal Support for the Visual Arts: The New Deal and Now*

Analyze Sources

According to Bufano, how was the FAP benefiting society?

HISTORICAL SOURCE 5

A Monthly Check to You

When the Social Security system was established in 1935, the government distributed posters to familiarize Americans with the benefits of Social Security. This poster was printed in 1936 during the initial issuance of social security numbers at U.S. post offices.

Analyze Sources

How does the Social Security poster illustrate how the federal government assumed some responsibility for the social welfare of citizens?

World War II
Document-Based Investigation

Part 1: Short Answer

In this module, you will analyze several historical documents. Carefully read or examine each document. Then answer the question that follows, citing text evidence where appropriate.

Part 2: Write an Analytical Essay

Historical Context

World War II began in 1939 when Germany invaded and tried to annex Poland, but the conflict quickly spread through the rest of the world. Within a few years, fighting had consumed huge expanses of Europe, Africa, and Asia. Millions of Americans sailed across the Atlantic and the Pacific to join the war, but the conflict's effects were felt even across the ocean at home.

Task

The violence of World War II destroyed communities and lives throughout Europe, Africa, and Asia, but people around the world felt its effects. Everyone—soldier and civilian, at home or abroad—sacrificed and struggled to meet the war's demands. Write an essay in which you analyze the effects of the war on various groups of people. Focus on three different groups, and explain their involvement in the war effort and how it changed their lives.

Complete the following steps as you plan and compose your analytical essay.

1. Review your notes and sources before you start writing.

2. Use at least *four* of the sources in Part 1, and develop the topic with relevant, well-chosen evidence from the documents.

3. Cite specific evidence from each of the sources in your response.

4. Plan your analytical essay so that it includes an introduction, body paragraphs with supporting details, and a concluding paragraph.

5. Organize your essay in a clear and logical way that presents a detailed analysis of the topic.

6. Write a conclusion that sums up your ideas and supports the information you present.

World War II

The London Blitz

Londoner Len Jones was just 18 years old when bombs fell on his East End neighborhood.

• •

"[T]he suction and the compression from the high-explosive bombs just pushed you and pulled you, and the whole of the atmosphere was turbulating so hard that, after an explosion of a nearby bomb, you could actually feel your eyeballs being [almost] sucked out . . . and the suction was so vast, it ripped my shirt away, and ripped my trousers. Then I couldn't get my breath, the smoke was like acid and everything round me was black and yellow. And these bombers kept on and on, the whole road was moving, rising and falling . . . ."

—Len Jones

quoted in *The Blitz: The British Under Attack*

Analyze Sources

How do you think the Blitz might have affected civilian morale in London?

HISTORICAL SOURCE 2

Concentration Camp Uniforms

Prisoners were required to wear color-coded triangles on their uniforms. There were several categories of prisoners. They included communists, socialists, criminals, emigrants, Jehovah's Witnesses, and homosexuals. They also included Germans and other nationalities "shy of work." The categories show a variation among the rows. One row is for repeat offenders, and one is for prisoners assigned to punish other prisoners. The double triangles are for Jews. Letters on top of a patch indicate nationality.

• •

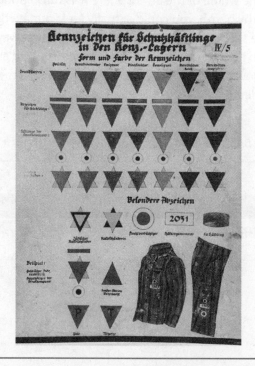

Analyze Sources

Why do you think the Nazis established this color-coded system to identify prisoners in the concentration camps?

HISTORICAL SOURCE   3

"The Only Way We Can Save Her"

During the late 1930s Americans watched events in Europe with alarm. Dictators were destroying democratic governments throughout Europe and dragging the continent into war. These events divided American public opinion. Some felt that the United States should help. Others opposed getting involved.

· ·

The character of Uncle Sam represents the government of the United States.

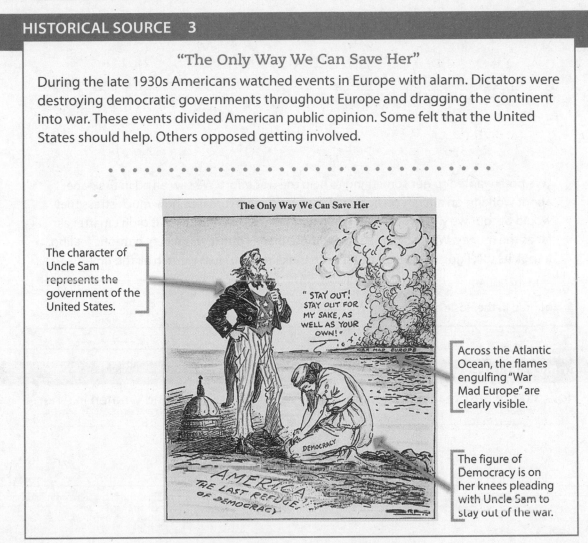

The Only Way We Can Save Her

" STAY OUT! STAY OUT FOR MY SAKE, AS WELL AS YOUR OWN!"

WAR MAD EUROPE

DEMOCRACY

AMERICA, THE LAST REFUGE OF DEMOCRACY

Across the Atlantic Ocean, the flames engulfing "War Mad Europe" are clearly visible.

The figure of Democracy is on her knees pleading with Uncle Sam to stay out of the war.

Analyze Sources

What does the kneeling figure fear will happen to America if Uncle Sam gets involved?

HISTORICAL SOURCE 4

Women in the Workplace

After the bombing of Pearl Harbor many women, barred from serving in the military, took jobs to support the war effort. Among those women were Mary Cohen of New York City and her sister.

• •

"We both wanted to get something to help the war effort. We saw an ad in the paper about working on aircraft on fighter planes. . . . We didn't realize how much stress that would be, but we were young, so it didn't bother us at that time. . . . It didn't matter as far as the money. We just wanted to get these planes out. It was a very patriotic feeling. It took its toll. I got sick once. I never even took time off. I just went in all the time."

—Mary Cohen

quoted in the Rosie the Riveter WWII Oral History Project

Analyze Sources

How did the outbreak of war change the lives of Mary Cohen and women like her?

HISTORICAL SOURCE   5

Stalingrad Prisoners of War

Dazed, starved, and freezing, these German soldiers were taken prisoner after months of struggle. But they were the lucky ones. More than 230,000 of their comrades died in the Battle of Stalingrad.

Analyze Sources

What does the photograph tell you about the conditions faced by the German soldiers at the Battle of Stalingrad? What details in the photograph support your conclusions?

HISTORICAL SOURCE 6

The Island of Death

When the Japanese left Guadalcanal, they called it the Island of Death. To war correspondent Ralph Martin and the troops who fought there, it was simply "hell."

• •

"Hell was red furry spiders as big as your fist, giant lizards as long as your leg, leeches falling from trees to suck blood, armies of white ants with a bite of fire, scurrying scorpions inflaming any flesh they touched, enormous rats and bats everywhere, and rivers with waiting crocodiles. Hell was the sour, foul smell of the squishy jungle, humidity that rotted a body within hours, . . . stinking wet heat of dripping rain forests that sapped the strength of any man."

—Ralph G. Martin

from *The GI War*

Analyze Sources

How might the conditions that Martin describes have affected the soldiers fighting there?

HISTORICAL SOURCE   7

A Shifting Population

Over 1.2 million African Americans left the South during World War II and the years that followed. Most of them moved to cities in the North and West in search of better jobs.

Analyze Sources

How did the wartime economy contribute to this mass migration?

The Cold War
Document-Based Investigation

Part 1: Short Answer

In this module, you will analyze several historical documents. Carefully read or examine each document. Then answer the question that follows, citing text evidence where appropriate.

Part 2: Write a Compare-and-Contrast Essay

Historical Context

Elected officials in the United States during the Cold War expressed a variety of reactions to the perceived threat of communism. Some called for increasing the country's arsenal and waging direct war against Communist nations. Others saw communism as a domestic problem that threatened to undermine American democracy and sought to root out the evil at home. Still others saw the Communists as political rivals who could nonetheless be negotiated with. These reactions and others helped shape American domestic and foreign policies during the Cold War.

Task

During the Cold War, communism was widely considered the greatest possible threat to the American way of life. Politicians devoted their lives to opposing the spread of communism, both at home and abroad. Write an essay comparing and contrasting the approaches taken by various officials in their fight against the Communist threat.

Complete the following steps as you plan and compose your compare-and-contrast essay.

Review your notes and sources before you start writing.

1. Use at least *four* of the sources in Part 1, and develop the topic with relevant, well-chosen evidence from the documents.

2. Cite specific evidence from each of the sources in your response.

3. Plan your compare-and-contrast essay so that it includes an introduction, several body paragraphs, and a concluding paragraph.

4. Organize your essay in a clear and logical way that highlights the similarities and differences among sources.

5. Write a conclusion that sums up your ideas and supports the information you present.

The Cold War

HISTORICAL SOURCE   1

The Truman Doctrine

In a 1947 speech to Congress, President Truman announced a significant change in U.S. foreign policy. With isolation no longer feasible and communism posing a threat around the world, Truman explained why he supported taking action to contain Soviet influence.

• •

"I believe that it must be the policy of the United States to support free peoples who are resisting attempted subjugation by armed minorities or by outside pressures.

I believe that we must assist free peoples to work out their own destinies in their own way.

I believe that our help should be primarily through economic and financial aid which is essential to economic stability and orderly political processes. . . .

Collapse of free institutions and loss of independence would be disastrous not only for them but for the world. Discouragement and possibly failure would quickly be the lot of neighboring peoples striving to maintain their freedom and independence. . . ."

—Harry S. Truman

from a speech to a joint session of Congress, March 12, 1947

Analyze Sources

How does Truman intend to help other countries resist Communist influence?

HISTORICAL SOURCE 2

"It's OK—We're Hunting Communists"

The fear of Communist subversion affected the entire society. People were so suspicious that almost any unusual opinion might be labeled "un-American." The climate of suspicion was most severe in the years 1947–1954, but it lasted throughout the 1950s.

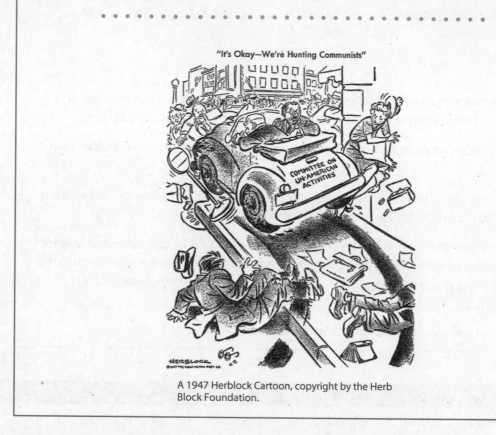

A 1947 Herblock Cartoon, copyright by the Herb Block Foundation.

Analyze Sources

What does the cartoon imply about the methods of HUAC?

HISTORICAL SOURCE 3

Effects of the Arms Race

As the United States and the Soviet Union rushed to produce nuclear weapons, many civilians lived in fear of a catastrophic attack. Eisenhower's policies of retaliation and brinkmanship heightened those fears. Across the country, civil defense agencies tried to prepare people for how to survive in the case of such an attack.

Analyze Sources

How does this poster reflect Americans' increased fears of conflict with the Soviet Union?

HISTORICAL SOURCE   4

Ich Bin ein Berliner

Two years after the construction of the Berlin Wall, President Kennedy traveled to West Berlin to renew his commitment to the city. In a famous speech, he praised the spirit of the city's people and declared the Berlin Wall a symbol of communism's weakness.

• •

"There are many people who really don't understand, or say they don't, what is the great issue between the free world and the Communist world. Let them come to Berlin. There are some who say that communism is the wave of the future. Let them come to Berlin. And there are some who say in Europe and elsewhere we can work with the Communists. Let them come to Berlin. . . . When all are free, then we can look forward to that day when this city will be joined as one. . . . All free men, wherever they may live, are citizens of Berlin, and, therefore, as a free man, I take pride in the words 'Ich bin ein Berliner!'"

—John F. Kennedy

from a speech in Berlin, June 26, 1963

Analyze Sources

What does Kennedy seek to accomplish by calling himself a Berliner?

┌───┐
│   │
│   │
│   │
│   │
│   │
└───┘

HISTORICAL SOURCE 5

Kissinger on Détente

Under President Richard Nixon and Secretary of State Henry Kissinger, the focus of U.S. foreign policy shifted from containment to détente. Kissinger offered a clear explanation of what this policy meant while visiting China in 1975.

• •

"The differences between us are apparent. Our task is not to intensify those differences. Our task is to advance our relationship on the basis of our mutual interests. Such a relationship would strengthen each of us. It would threaten no one and it would contribute to the well-being of all peoples. . . . Each country must pursue a policy suitable to its own circumstances. . . . In this policy we will be guided by actions and realities and not rhetoric."

—Henry Kissinger

from a toast to Chinese officials, October 19, 1975

Analyze Sources

How does Kissinger's description of détente differ from earlier Cold War foreign policies?

The Postwar Boom
Document-Based Investigation

Part 1: Short Answer

In this module, you will analyze several historical documents. Carefully read or examine each document. Then answer the question that follows, citing text evidence where appropriate.

Part 2: Deliver a Presentation

Historical Context

For many Americans the 1950s was a time of economic prosperity. As the majority of Americans began to make more money, they also began to change the way they lived. These changes—such as where they lived, how they felt about work and their roles in society, and what they spent their money on—had a ripple effect on American culture. Affluent and middle-class families moved to the suburbs to create new lives, leaving the cities behind. This mainstream culture valued conformity, and for the most part, they turned a blind eye to the populations who did not fit the mold they were creating for themselves.

Task

As the mainstream culture changed in a way that encouraged conformity, a subculture rose up to reject those values. Create a presentation that explains the factors that led to cultural changes in the 1950s and the effect those changes had on American society as a whole.

Complete the following steps as you plan and prepare your presentation.

1. Review your notes and sources before you start writing.

2. Use at least *three* of the sources in Part 1, and develop the topic with relevant, well-chosen evidence from the documents.

3. Cite specific evidence from each of the sources in your response.

4. Plan your presentation so that information is delivered clearly and logically to the audience.

5. Speak clearly and with enough volume to be heard, employ relevant visuals, and use presentation technology as applicable.

6`. Conclude with a summation of the main points of your presentation.

The Postwar Boom

A Dynamic Economy

Following World War II, the United States experienced an unprecedented economic boom. Employment increased, and consumers—forced to skimp and sacrifice during the war—were eager to spend some of their new income.

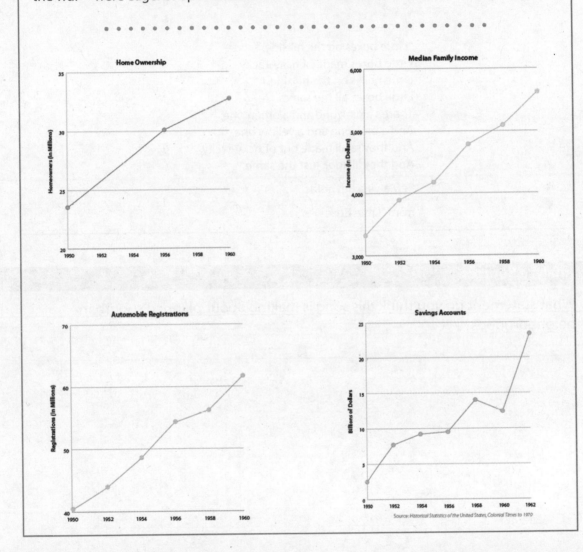

Source: Historical Statistics of the United States, Colonial Times to 1970

Analyze Sources

What would explain the slow growth in savings between 1952 and 1958?

HISTORICAL SOURCE   2

"Little Boxes"

In a popular protest song, Malvina Reynolds sings about boxes lining a hillside. She is referring to the suburban housing developments that were planned and built in the 1950s. Ticky-tacky is the cheap, shoddy building material that was used to construct the homes. The song continues to say that the people who live in the boxes are also "all made out of ticky-tacky" and "all look just the same."

• •

"Little boxes on the hillside,
Little boxes made of ticky-tacky,
Little boxes on the hillside,
Little boxes all the same.
There's a pink one and a green one,
And a blue one and a yellow one,
And they're all made out of ticky-tacky,
And they all look just the same."

—Malvina Reynolds

from "Little Boxes"

Analyze Sources

What statement do you think this song is making about planned suburban neighborhoods?

HISTORICAL SOURCE 3

The Beatniks

Jack Kerouac and other writers of the beat movement took the position of outsiders, writing about nonconformist lifestyles.

• •

"They danced down the streets like dingledodies, and I shambled after as I've been doing all my life after people who interest me, because the only people for me are the mad ones, the ones who are mad to live, mad to talk, mad to be saved, desirous of everything at the same time, the ones that never yawn or say a commonplace thing, but burn, burn, burn like fabulous yellow roman candles exploding like spiders across the stars. . . ."

—Jack Kerouac

from *On the Road*

Analyze Sources

Why do you think Kerouac's writing style appealed to teenagers and college students? How do you think it made them feel?

HISTORICAL SOURCE   4

Poverty in America

In 1962 Michael Harrington published *The Other America: Poverty in the United States,* revealing the realities of widespread poverty.

· ·

"The poor get sick more than anyone else in the society. . . . When they become sick, they are sick longer than any other group in the society. Because they are sick more often and longer than anyone else, they lose wages and work, and find it difficult to hold a steady job. And because of this, they cannot pay for good housing, for a nutritious diet, for doctors."

—Michael Harrington

from *The Other America*

Analyze Sources

How do you think middle-class, suburban Americans felt when reading Harrington's descriptions of the poor and their struggles?

An Era of Social Change
Document-Based Investigation

Part 1: Short Answer

In this module, you will analyze several historical documents. Carefully read or examine each document. Then answer the question that follows, citing text evidence where appropriate.

Part 2: Write an Explanatory Essay

Historical Context

Following the election of 1960, many Americans felt a strong sense of hope that the country was entering into an era of progress. Many social issues plagued the country—including prejudice against African Americans that led to injustices and inequalities. And despite widespread prosperity, millions of Americans lived in poverty. Kennedy and Johnson both championed public service and vowed that their administrations would work with Congress to pass legislation that would bring about sweeping social change. Meanwhile, social movements were stirring that would band together to call for change and ask the government to take further action.

Task

The 1960s and 1970s saw many social changes. Write an explanatory essay that explains the impact that elected officials such as the president and members of congress can have on social issues, such as racism, poverty, and/or environmental protection. You may choose one social issue to focus on or you may use more than one social issue to help explain your points.

Complete the following steps as you plan and compose your explanatory essay.

1. Review your notes and sources before you start writing.

2. Use at least *three* of the sources in Part 1, and develop the topic with relevant, well-chosen evidence from the documents.

3. Cite specific evidence from each of the sources in your response.

4. Plan your explanatory essay so that it includes an introduction, several body paragraphs, and a concluding paragraph.

5. Organize your essay in a clear and logical way that provides a detailed explanation of the topic.

6. Write a conclusion that sums up your ideas and supports the information you present.

An Era of Social Change

The Great Society Speech

Speaking at the University of Michigan, President Johnson told an enthusiastic crowd that he envisioned a legislative program that would create not only a higher standard of living and equal opportunity but also promote a richer quality of life for all.

• •

"The Great Society is a place where every child can find knowledge to enrich his mind and to enlarge his talents. It is a place where leisure is a welcome chance to build and reflect, not a feared cause of boredom and restlessness. It is a place where the city of man serves not only the needs of the body and the demands of commerce but the desire for beauty and the hunger for community. It is a place where man can renew contact with nature. It is a place which honors creation for its own sake and for what it adds to the understanding of the race."

—Lyndon B. Johnson

from "The Great Society," May 22, 1964

Analyze Sources

How did President Johnson use language to inspire Americans to share his vision?

HISTORICAL SOURCE 2

Bob Dylan's Music

Although Bob Dylan did not claim to be a spokesperson for his generation, millions of Americans felt his songs perfectly expressed their frustrations, fears, and hopes. In 1999 *Time* magazine included Dylan in its "Time 100: The Most Important People of the Century."

. . . .

"Come senators, congressmen
Please heed the call
Don't stand in the doorway
Don't block up the hall
For he that gets hurt
Will be he who has stalled
There's a battle outside
And it is ragin'.
It'll soon shake your windows
And rattle your walls
For the times they are a-changin'."

—Bob Dylan

from "The Times They Are A-Changin'," 1962

Analyze Sources

How might listeners of different ages and cultures have responded to these lyrics?

HISTORICAL SOURCE 3

Clean Air Poster

President Nixon created the EPA in 1970 by signing the National Environmental Policy Act (NEPA). A major element of the NEPA is the requirement that an environmental impact statement (EIS) be prepared for all major federal actions that might significantly affect the environment.

• •

Analyze Sources

What does the poster imply about the role of governmental regulations?

Civil Rights
Document-Based Investigation

Part 1: Short Answer

In this module, you will analyze several historical documents. Carefully read or examine each document. Then answer the question that follows, citing text evidence where appropriate.

Part 2: Write an Explanatory Essay

Historical Context

As the 1960s began, southern civil rights leaders called for new efforts in the struggle for racial equality. These efforts won passage of important civil rights and voting rights laws in 1964 and 1965, but some young members of the movement believed that progress was too slow. In the mid-1960s, frustration over the lack of progress exploded into violence. Meanwhile other groups, inspired by African American activism, fought for equal rights using a variety of methods.

Task

Activists use a wide range of tools and methods to get attention and results. Write an essay in which you present and explain methods used by leaders during the civil rights movement as well as leaders of the movements it inspired.

Complete the following steps as you plan and compose your explanatory essay.

1. Review your notes and sources before you start writing.

2. Use at least *four* of the sources in Part 1, and develop the topic with relevant, well-chosen evidence from the documents.

3. Cite specific evidence from each of the sources in your response.

4. Plan your explanatory essay so that it includes an introduction, several body paragraphs, and a concluding paragraph.

5. Organize your essay in a clear and logical way that provides a detailed explanation of the topic.

6. Write a conclusion that sums up your ideas and supports the information you present.

Civil Rights

Sit-Ins

Sit-in demonstrators, such as these at a Jackson, Mississippi, lunch counter in 1963, faced intimidation and humiliation from white segregationists.

• •

Analyze Sources

What does this photograph tell you about how many whites in the South felt about equal rights for African Americans? What can you tell about the protesters sitting at the counter?

HISTORICAL SOURCE   2

Capturing the Movement

Born in Memphis in 1922, photographer Ernest Withers believed that if the struggle for equality could be shown to people, things would change. Armed with only a camera, he braved violent crowds to capture the heated racism during the Montgomery bus boycott, the desegregation of Central High in Little Rock, and the 1968 Memphis sanitation workers strike—shown in this photograph—led by Martin Luther King Jr. The night before the Memphis march, Withers helped make some of the signs he photographed.

Analyze Sources

What do the signs tell you about African Americans' struggle for civil rights? What kind of treatment do you suppose these men had experienced? Why do you think so?

HISTORICAL SOURCE 3

Black Power

Stokely Carmichael was arrested in Greenwood, Mississippi, during the march to complete Meredith's walk. When he showed up at a rally later, his face swollen from a beating, he electrified the crowd.

• •

"This is the twenty-seventh time I have been arrested—and I ain't going to jail no more! The only way we're gonna stop them white men from whippin' us is to take over. We been saying freedom for six years—and we ain't got nothin'. What we gonna start now is BLACK POWER."

—Stokely Carmichael

quoted in *The Civil Rights Movement: An Eyewitness History*

Analyze Sources

Why do you think Carmichael's message appealed to many African Americans?

Labor Unions

César Chávez firmly believed that unionization was the best way to improve working conditions and wages.

. . . .

"The need is for amendments that will make strong, effective labor unions realistically possible in agriculture. I say 'realistically possible' because laws cannot deliver a good union any more than laws can bring an end to poverty. Only people can do that through hard work, sacrifice and dedicated effort. . . . Our cause, our strike and our international boycott are all founded upon the deep conviction that the form of collective self-help which is unionization holds far more hope for the farm worker than any other single approach, . . . The best insurance against strikes and boycotts lies not in repressive legislation, but in strong unions that will satisfy the farmworker's hunger for decency and dignity and self-respect. Unionization cannot make progress in the face of hostile employer attitudes unless it receives effective governmental support."

—César Chávez

quoted from a speech before the Senate Subcommittee on Labor, April 16, 1969

Analyze Sources

What role does Chávez hope that the government will play in labor relations?

Document-Based Investigation Workbook

HISTORICAL SOURCE   5

Ms. Magazine

In 1972 Gloria Steinem and other women created a new women's magazine, *Ms.*, designed to treat contemporary issues from a feminist perspective. On the cover of this 1972 issue of *Ms.*, the woman shown has eight arms and is holding a different object in each hand.

Analyze Sources

What do you think these objects symbolize in terms of women's roles? What do you think this drawing says about women in the 1960s? Explain.

HISTORICAL SOURCE   6

Americans with Disabilities Act

On July 26, 1990, President George H. W. Bush signed the Americans with Disabilities Act into law. He spoke to the crowd gathered on the White House lawn about the importance of the act and the new freedoms it would provide.

• •

"With today's signing of the landmark Americans [with] Disabilities Act, every man, woman, and child with a disability can now pass through once-closed doors into a bright new era of equality, independence, and freedom. . . . I remember clearly how many years of dedicated commitment have gone into making this historic new civil rights act a reality. It's been the work of a true coalition, a strong and inspiring coalition of people who have shared both a dream and a passionate determination to make that dream come true . . . a joining of Democrats and Republicans, of the legislative and the executive branches, of Federal and State agencies, of public officials and private citizens, of people with disabilities and without.

This act . . . will ensure that people with disabilities are given the basic guarantees for which they have worked so long and so hard: independence, freedom of choice, control of their lives, the opportunity to blend fully and equally into the rich mosaic of the American mainstream. Legally, it will provide our disabled community with a powerful expansion of protections . . . It will guarantee fair and just access to the fruits of American life which we all must be able to enjoy."

—George H. W. Bush

from a speech on July 26, 1990

Analyze Sources

Explain why it takes a coalition such as the groups President Bush lists to create a new civil rights law.

Name _____ Class _____ Date _____

Part 1: Short Answer

In this module, you will analyze several historical documents. Carefully read or examine each document. Then answer the question that follows, citing text evidence where appropriate.

Part 2: Write an Explanatory Essay

Historical Context

The United States' aims in the Vietnam War were similar to its aims in World War II—to protect democracy. Yet many Americans' feelings about the United States' involvement in Vietnam were vastly different than those frequently expressed during World War II and other wars. While people generally consider World War II a clear and just fight against evil, the justifications for the Vietnam War were less obvious to many Americans.

Task

Write an essay in which you summarize the United States' reasons for entering the two wars, and explain why public support for the Vietnam War was split more so than it was during World War II.

Complete the following steps as you plan and compose your explanatory essay.

1. Review your notes and sources before you start writing.

2. Use at least *four* of the sources in Part 1, and develop the topic with relevant, well-chosen evidence from the documents.

3. Cite specific evidence from each of the sources in your response.

4. Plan your explanatory essay so that it includes an introduction, several body paragraphs, and a concluding paragraph.

5. Organize your essay in a clear and logical way that provides a detailed explanation of the topic.

6. Write a conclusion that sums up your ideas and supports the information you present.

The Vietnam War

War or Peace?

This photograph of a U.S. soldier wearing symbols of both war and peace illustrates how many U.S. soldiers struggled with their role in Vietnam. They were required to serve, but many wanted peace, not war.

• •

Analyze Sources

How does the photograph reflect Americans' feelings about the war in Vietnam?

HISTORICAL SOURCE 2

Johnson Remains Determined

President Johnson faced criticism on both sides of the war debate. Doves criticized him for not withdrawing from Vietnam. Hawks accused him of not increasing military power rapidly enough. Johnson was dismissive of both groups and their motives. He defended his reasons for continuing his policy of slow escalation.

• •

"We made our statement to the world of what we would do if we had Communist aggression in that part of the world in 1954. . . . We said we would stand with those people in the face of common danger. . . . Every country that I know in that area that is familiar with what is happening thinks it is absolutely essential that Uncle Sam keep his word and stay there until we can find an honorable peace. . . . There has always been confusion, frustration, and difference of opinion in this country when there is a war going on. . . . We are going to have these differences. No one likes war. All people love peace. But you can't have freedom without defending it."

—Lyndon B. Johnson

from a press conference, November 17, 1967

Analyze Sources

What are Johnson's justifications for continuing his policy of escalating U.S. involvement in Vietnam?

HISTORICAL SOURCE   3

Growing Doubts

Public criticism of the government's policies in Vietnam grew louder and more intense following the Tet offensive. Americans began to doubt that Communist forces were weakening and that the United States would soon win the war.

. . . .

Changing Opinions About the War

y-axis: Percentage of Americans Who Believed the Vietnam War Was a Mistake

70, 60, 50, 40, 30, 20, 10, 0

x-axis: 1965 1966 1967 1968 1969 1970 1971 1972 1973

Source: Pew Research Center

Analyze Sources

What is significant about the change in public opinion about the war from 1967 to 1968?

HISTORICAL SOURCE   4

Kent State Shooting

Photographer John Filo was a senior at Kent State University when antiwar demonstrations rocked the campus. When the National Guard began firing at student protesters, Filo began shooting pictures. Nixon and his supporters had been successful in characterizing student protesters as spoiled and destructive young people, not worthy of serious consideration. Filo's Pulitzer-prize winning photograph of Mary Ann Vecchio grieving over the body of Jeffery Glenn Miller changed these perceptions by suggesting that the students—who looked no different than other young people of the time—were undeserving of the brutal response of the National Guard.

• •

Analyze Sources

Why do you think this photograph remains a symbol of the Vietnam War era today?

Transitions and Conservatism
Document-Based Investigation

Part 1: Short Answer

In this module, you will analyze several historical documents. Carefully read or examine each document. Then answer the question that follows, citing text evidence where appropriate.

Part 2: Write a Compare-and-Contrast Essay

Historical Context

Upon election, President Nixon promised to restore order to a country plagued by urban riots and antiwar demonstrations. He also promised to turn the country in a more conservative direction. Although scandal derailed the Nixon presidency, the country began to slowly move in a more conservative direction. A weak economy and turmoil in the Middle East plague the Carter presidency, and in 1980 Ronald Reagan won election. As president, Reagan continued to push the conservative agenda, reducing the size of government and shifting the Supreme Court to the right.

Task

President Richard M. Nixon entered office in 1969 determined to turn America in a more conservative direction. One of the main items on President Nixon's agenda was to reduce the size and influence of the federal government. Nixon's plan, known as New Federalism, was to distribute a portion of federal power to state and local governments. In 1980, conservatives helped elect one of their own—Ronald Reagan—a true believer in less government, lower taxes, and traditional values. Reagan promised to restore Americans' faith in the presidency and start a "Reagan revolution." Write an essay comparing the Nixon Administration to the Reagan Administration to describe how each was able to implement the goals of the conservative movement.

Complete the following steps as you plan and compose your compare-and-contrast essay.

1. Review your notes and sources before you start writing.

2. Use at least *four* of the sources in Part 1, and develop the topic with relevant, well-chosen evidence from the documents.

3. Cite specific evidence from each of the sources in your response.

4. Plan your compare-and-contrast essay so that it includes an introduction, several body paragraphs, and a concluding paragraph.

5. Organize your essay in a clear and logical way that highlights the similarities and differences among sources.

6. Write a conclusion that sums up your ideas and supports the information you present.

Transitions and Conservatism

HISTORICAL SOURCE   1

"Domestic Life"

Pulitzer Prize–winning cartoonist Paul Szep frequently used Nixon as the subject of his cartoons. The cartoonist uses a famous nursery rhyme to illustrate Nixon's focus on foreign policy over domestic policy.

The shoe in which Old Mother Hubbard and her many children live is labeled Domestic Programs.

Old Mother Hubbard's many hungry, poor children— representing various domestic social programs—are crying for their mother as she leaves through the gate.

President Richard Nixon is portrayed here as the nursery rhyme character Old Mother Hubbard.

Analyze Sources

What does the cartoonist suggest about Nixon by showing him leaving with his bags packed?

Document-Based Investigation Workbook

HISTORICAL SOURCE   2

The White House Tapes

During the Watergate hearings, a bombshell exploded when it was revealed that President Nixon secretly tape-recorded all conversations in the Oval Office. Although Nixon hoped the tapes would one day help historians document the triumphs of his presidency, they were used to confirm his guilt.

Analyze Sources

What does this cartoon imply about privacy during President Nixon's term in office?

Document-Based Investigation Workbook

HISTORICAL SOURCE 3

Energy Crisis

On April 18, 1977, during a fireside chat, Carter urged his fellow Americans to cut their consumption of oil and gas.

• •

"The energy crisis . . . is a problem . . . likely to get progressively worse through the rest of this century. . . . Our decision about energy will test the character of the American people. . . . This difficult effort will be the 'moral equivalent of war,' except that we will be uniting our efforts to build and not to destroy."

—Jimmy Carter

quoted in *Keeping Faith*

Analyze Sources

What do you think Carter means by comparing the energy crisis to war?

HISTORICAL SOURCE 4

Moral Majority

The Moral Majority worked toward their political goals by using direct-mail campaigns to reach voters and by raising money to support candidates. In 1980 Reverend Jerry Falwell wrote a book in which he explained the motivations behind the actions of the Moral Majority.

· ·

"Our nation's internal problems are the direct result of her spiritual condition. . . . Right living must be reestablished as an American way of life. . . . Now is the time to begin calling America back to God, back to the Bible, back to morality."

—Reverend Jerry Falwell

From *Listen, America!*

Analyze Sources

How did Jerry Falwell propose that the country fix its social problems?

HISTORICAL SOURCE 5

Deficit Spending

During Reagan's first term, federal spending far outstripped federal revenue and created a huge budget deficit. In this cartoon, Reagan (with budget director David Stockman sitting beside him on the "Inflation" stagecoach) sees something that "shouldn't be there."

Analyze Sources

Whom do the passengers inside the stagecoach represent?

HISTORICAL SOURCE 6

Iran-Contra Affair

President Reagan's message to television audiences about selling arms to Iran differed greatly from what was going on behind the scenes.

"Arms payoff for hostage release," a 1986 Herblock Cartoon, copyright by the Herb Block Foundation.

Analyze Sources

What does the cartoon accuse President Reagan of doing?

Into a New Millennium
Document-Based Investigation

Part 1: Short Answer

In this module, you will analyze several historical documents. Carefully read or examine each document. Then answer the question that follows, citing text evidence where appropriate.

Part 2: Write an Argument

Historical Context

Tumultuous events marked the period from the early 1990s to about 2015, from acts of terrorism to war to remarkable advances in science and technology.

Task

As the 20th century came to a close and the 21st began, along with the era's many changes were shifts in how Americans felt about each other. Write an argument in which you claim that Americans either drew closer together during this period or that they pulled further apart.

Complete the following steps as you plan and compose your argument.

1. Review your notes and sources before you start writing.

2. Use at least *four* of the sources in Part 1, and develop the topic with relevant, well-chosen evidence from the documents.

3. Cite specific evidence from each of the sources in your response.

4. Plan your argument so that it includes an introduction, body paragraphs with supporting details, and a concluding paragraph.

5. Organize your argument in a clear and logical way that expresses your point of view to the reader.

6. Write a conclusion that sums up your ideas and supports the information you present.

Name _____ Class _____ Date _____

Into a New Millennium

Outsourcing

Economic globalization created both problems and opportunities. Outsourcing was one unfortunate result.

· ·

"The last step says to dismantle the whole thing
and ship all the jobs overseas."

Analyze Sources

How does this cartoon illustrate changes in employment patterns?

HISTORICAL SOURCE   2

Knowns and Unknowns

Whether or not Iraq still controlled WMD became a hot topic, including at a news briefing where Secretary of Defense Donald Rumsfeld described the difficulty of learning the truth.

· ·

"Reports that say that something hasn't happened are always interesting to me, because as we know, there are known knowns; there are things we know we know. We also know there are known unknowns; that is to say we know there are some things we do not know. But there are also unknown unknowns—the ones we don't know we don't know. And if one looks throughout the history of our country and other free countries, it is the latter category that tend to be the difficult ones."

—Donald Rumsfeld

from a Department of Defense hearing, February 2002

Analyze Sources

Why do you think Rumsfeld's comments were both criticized and praised? With which stance do you agree, and why?

HISTORICAL SOURCE 3

Tension and Triumph

At 11:35 p.m. on May 1, 2011, President Obama announced that Osama bin Laden had been found in his Pakistan compound and killed, along with several other residents. Several groups contributed to the operation—the CIA, U.S. Naval Special Warfare Development Group (known as SEAL Team Six), and U.S. Army Special Operations Command's 160th Special Operations Aviation Regiment (Airborne). There were no American casualties. This photo shows President Obama, key Cabinet members, and other advisers at the White House watching the take-down unfold.

Analyze Sources

How do you think this photo, which represented the mission to eliminate bin Laden, affected most Americans?

HISTORICAL SOURCE   4

"Vacation, 2000"

By the end of the 20th century, millions of Americans owned any number of personal communication devices. People were able to speak to or correspond with each other instantaneously almost anytime, almost anywhere.

Analyze Sources

What does the cartoon suggest about Americans and their communication devices? Do you agree or disagree with the cartoonist's message? Explain your opinion.

HISTORICAL SOURCE 5

The Graying of America

Because life expectancy has increased, the U.S. population is aging. Sociologists anticipate that the elderly will make up a larger percentage of the population in the near future, as the projected figures on the table below show.

• •

The Graying of America, 1990–2030

Year	Number of Americans 65 and Older	Percent of American Population
1990	31,081,000	12.4
2000	34,837,000	12.7
2010	40,229,000	13.0
2020	54,804,000	16.1
2030	72,092,000	19.3

Source: *2010 Statistical Abstract of the United States (online)*

Analyze Sources

Between what years is America's elderly population expected to grow the most? By roughly what percentage is America's elderly population expected to increase between 1990 and 2030?

The United States in the 21st Century
Document-Based Investigation

Part 1: Short Answer

In this module, you will analyze several historical documents. Carefully read or examine each document. Then answer the question that follows, citing text evidence where appropriate.

Part 2: Write an Argument

Historical Context

In the first years of the 21st century, Americans have confronted daunting issues on the domestic and global fronts. Voices of both doom and inspiration fight for attention.

Task

The challenges that lie ahead are considerable, but not insurmountable. How effectively will the country confront them? Write an argument in which you discuss how well you think the American people are prepared for the challenges of the 21st century.

Complete the following steps as you plan and compose your argument.

1. Review your notes and sources before you start writing.

2. Use at least *four* of the sources in Part 1, and develop the topic with relevant, well-chosen evidence from the documents.

3. Cite specific evidence from each of the sources in your response.

4. Plan your argument so that it includes an introduction, body paragraphs with supporting details, and a concluding paragraph.

5. Organize your argument in a clear and logical way that expresses your point of view to the reader.

6. Write a conclusion that sums up your ideas and supports the information you present.

The United States in the 21st Century

Radicals and the Internet

Security officials are facing new challenges in their efforts to keep Americans safe. During a U.S. Senate hearing, the witnesses were asked what keeps them awake at night. Following is FBI Director Robert Mueller's response.

• •

"[I]t is the radicalization of individuals on the Internet, who develop the desire and the will to undertake attacks. They're finding it very difficult to find co-conspirators, others that would join in. But then again, the Internet can facilitate that kind of a meeting/ coming together for an attack. And it is the lone wolves that we are principally concerned about."

—Robert Mueller

from testimony before the U.S. Senate Select Committee on Intelligence, March 12, 2013

Analyze Sources

How does the Internet affect the spread of radical ideas?

HISTORICAL SOURCE   2

An East Asian Threat

Kim Jong Un rules North Korea as a militaristic dictatorship. The people there have few freedoms, and many struggle to survive. Yet North Korea—also known as the DPRK, or Democratic People's Republic of Korea—has a huge and powerful military program, as described by the CIA's *World Factbook*.

• •

"After decades of economic mismanagement and resource misallocation [misuse], the DPRK since the mid-1990s has relied heavily on international aid to feed its population. The DPRK began to ease restrictions to allow semi-private markets, starting in 2002, but then sought to roll back the scale of economic reforms in 2005 and 2009. North Korea's history of regional military provocations; proliferation of military-related items; long-range missile development; WMD programs including tests of nuclear devices in 2006, 2009, and 2013; and massive conventional armed forces are of major concern to the international community. The regime in 2013 announced a new policy calling for the simultaneous development of the North's nuclear weapons program and its economy."

—Central Intelligence Agency

from *The World Factbook*, 2015

Analyze Sources

What special problems does North Korea present for U.S. diplomacy?

HISTORICAL SOURCE   3

The Income Gap

Although Americans' incomes have, in general, increased in the last few decades, the disparity among the gains of various economic groups is dramatic.

• •

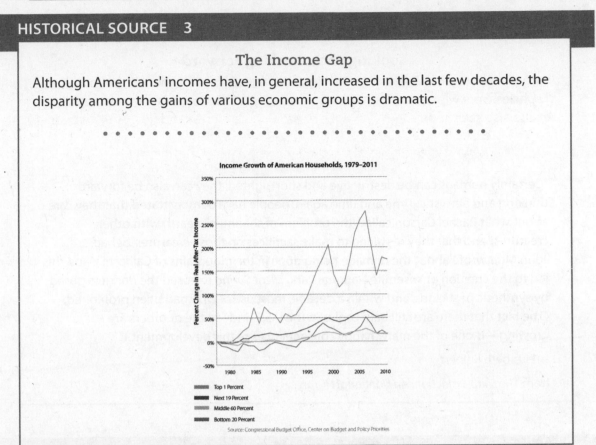

Income Growth of American Households, 1979–2011

Source: Congressional Budget Office, Center on Budget and Policy Priorities

Analyze Sources

Which group's income had increased by more than 250 percent by about 2005? Of the other groups, which experienced the greatest fluctuation in income growth?

HISTORICAL SOURCE 4

Looking Back, Looking Forward

Journalist Elizabeth Kolbert reviewed the times in Earth's history when vast numbers of species were wiped out. She sees human beings as the cause of the next cataclysm. Yet she also sees hope.

• •

"Certainly humans can be destructive and shortsighted; they can also be forward-thinking and altruistic. Time and time again, people have demonstrated that they care about what Rachel Carson called 'the problem of sharing our earth with other creatures,' and that they're willing to make sacrifices on those creatures' behalf. . . . John Muir wrote about the damage being done in the mountains of California, and this led to the creation of Yosemite National Park. *Silent Spring* exposed the dangers posed by synthetic pesticides, and within a decade, most use of DDT had been prohibited. (The fact that there are still bald eagles in the U.S.—indeed the numbers are growing—is one of the many happy consequences of this development.)"

—Elizabeth Kolbert

from *The Sixth Extinction: An Unnatural History*

Analyze Sources

What gives Elizabeth Kolbert hope for America's future?

HISTORICAL SOURCE 5

Evaluating American Education

In a speech introducing his Race to the Top program, President Obama reviewed some of the problems facing the American educational system.

· ·

"In an economy where knowledge is the most valuable commodity a person and a country have to offer, the best jobs will go to the best educated—whether they live in the United States or India or China. In a world where countries that out-educate us today will out-compete us tomorrow, the future belongs to the nation that best educates its people. . . . But we also know that today, our education system is falling short. . . . The United States, a country that has always led the way in innovation, is now being outpaced in math and science education. African American, Latino students are lagging behind white classmates in one subject after another—an achievement gap that, by one estimate, costs us hundreds of billions of dollars in wages that will not be earned, jobs that will not be done, and purchases that will not be made. And most employers raise doubts about the qualifications of future employees, rating high school graduates' basic skills as only 'fair' or 'poor.'"

—Barack Obama

from a speech at the U.S. Department of Education, July 24, 2009

Analyze Sources

Do you think President Obama's assessment is accurate? Why or why not?

Name _____ Class _____ Date _____

HISTORICAL SOURCE 6

Evaluating Globalization

Joseph Stiglitz has been the chief economist for the World Bank and chair of President Clinton's Council of Economic Advisers. He has studied the issues resulting from globalization, including resulting environmental damage and the impact on many poor workers. In the quote below, Stiglitz addresses the question of how to solve these dilemmas.

• •

"To some, there is an easy answer: Abandon globalization. That is neither feasible nor desirable. . . . [G]lobalization has also brought huge benefits—East Asia's success was based on globalization, especially on the opportunities for trade, and increased access to markets and technology. Globalization has brought better health, as well as an active global civil society fighting for more democracy and greater social justice. The problem is not with globalization, but with how it has been managed. Part of the problem lies with the international economic institutions . . . which help set the rules of the game. They have done so in ways that, all too often, have served the interests of the more advanced industrialized countries—and particular interests within those countries—rather than those of the developing world."

—Joseph Stiglitz

quoted in *Globalization and Its Discontents*

Analyze Sources

What responsibility does the American public have for making globalization a force that helps rich and poor alike?